Robert Quackenbush

WHO LET MUDDY BOOTS INTO THE WHITE HOUSE?

A Story of Andrew Jackson

SIMON AND SCHUSTER BOOKS FOR YOUNG READERS
Published by Simon & Schuster Inc., New York

SIMON AND SCHUSTER
BOOKS FOR YOUNG READERS
Simon & Schuster Building
Rockefeller Center
1230 Avenue of the Americas
New York, New York 10020
SIMON AND SCHUSTER BOOKS FOR YOUNG READERS
is a trademark of Simon & Schuster Inc.
Printed in Spain

10 9 8 7 6 5 4 3 2

Library of Congress Cataloging-in-Publication Data
Quackenbush, Robert M.
  Who let muddy boots into the White House?
  SUMMARY: A humorous biography of the first "common
man" President, who was a hero of the War of 1812
and who represented the "new" America of the frontier.
   1. Jackson, Andrew, 1767–1845—Juvenile literature.
2. Presidents—United States—Biography—Juvenile
literature. [1. Jackson, Andrew, 1767–1845.
2. Presidents] I. Title.
E382.Q33 1986   973.5′6′0924 [B] [92] 86-4989
ISBN 0-671-66970-2

There once was a boy named Andrew Jackson. He was born on March 15, 1767, in a log cabin on the boundary line between North Carolina and South Carolina. Three weeks before Andrew was born, his father died. So his mother had to move to Andrew's aunt and uncle's house nearby. It was a noisy household filled with eleven children—Andrew, his two older brothers, and eight cousins. Being the youngest, Andrew grew up learning to fend for himself. He was a mischievous, red-haired boy who liked to play practical jokes and who was often in trouble. He got little education in the region where he lived, called the Waxhaws, and he never liked schoolwork. He preferred running free with his friends. As a result, his spelling was a wonder to behold. All his life he might spell the same word three or four different ways on a single page!

In spite of Andrew's poor education, he could read well enough. In 1776, when he was nine, he was chosen to read the Declaration of Independence in the town square to those who couldn't read. This exciting proclamation declared America's freedom from British rule, and it led to the Revolutionary War. But four years passed before the war came to the Waxhaws. The Jackson family had its full share of fighting and suffering. When the war was over, Andrew at age sixteen was an orphan. His brothers Hugh and Robert had died in the army. His mother had died of ship's fever while nursing American prisoners on British prison ships. Andrew himself had been captured by the British and held prisoner for a while. On his forehead was the mark of a sword blow from a British officer whose boots Andrew had refused to shine. None of this broke his spirit. He was still the most rollicking, mischievous fellow who ever lived.

10

When he was still only sixteen, Andrew received some money that was willed to him by his grandfather in Ireland. Friends told Andrew that $1500 was enough to buy a nice farm or to pay for a good education. However, Andrew thought he knew an easy way to make a lot more money. He went to Charleston, South Carolina, to bet on horse races, but after just one week of gambling, all the money—and more—was gone. It was a bitter lesson. Andrew never wanted to be burdened with debts again. But how could he be sure of earning money? Becoming a lawyer was the answer. It wouldn't take too long, since there wasn't so much to learn about the law as there is today. And many frontier lawyers became wealthy and famous, attracting crowds to the courtrooms to listen to their arguments. It was almost like a play. So Jackson found a lawyer in Salisbury, North Carolina, to teach him law.

13

ORDER IN THE COURT!

WHY DIDN'T ANDREW JACKSON GO TO LAW SCHOOL?

THERE WERE NO LAW SCHOOLS THEN. A YOUNG MAN WHO WANTED TO BECOME A LAWYER SIMPLY "READ LAW" WITH AN ESTABLISHED ATTORNEY UNTIL HE WAS ABLE TO PASS HIS BAR EXAMINATION.

Jackson lived in Salisbury until 1788, when he finished his education and became a lawyer. Then he got a job as the public prosecutor in the settlement of Nashville in Tennessee. His work would consist of keeping order and forcing people to pay their debts. Andrew rented a room in the home of Mrs. Donelson, whose husband Colonel Donelson had founded Nashville. The Colonel had recently died, and Mrs. Donelson took in male boarders to protect her and her family. Once settled, Jackson set to work. A rough bunch of men in Nashville had banded together and refused to pay their debts. They were not about to let a skinny 21-year-old prosecutor tell them what to do. It was up to Jackson to set them straight about the law, and in the process he got involved in a number of street fights. But once he succeeded, he got other work as a lawyer. Soon he was known as an important person in the community.

15

While he was living at Mrs. Donelson's, Jackson fell in love with one of her daughters, Rachel. Unfortunately, Rachel was already married to a man in Kentucky who treated her very badly. Jackson moved out of the house. Then he learned that Rachel's husband had divorced her. Without checking the details, he proposed to her and they were married in 1791. Two years later, Jackson discovered to his horror that the divorce had just become final. He and Rachel were not legally married. Quickly, they married again, but his mistake caused a scandal. People gossiped about them behind their backs. Jackson polished his dueling pistols—an accepted way of settling disputes in those rugged days—in case any man said something cruel about Rachel to his face. Twice he fought in duels and twice he was shot—once in his shoulder and once an inch above his heart. The bullet missed Jackson's heart only because he was so skinny under his loose-hanging jacket.

17

In 1796, when Tennessee was admitted as the 16th state, Jackson was asked to help write the state constitution. Then he was elected as Tennessee's first representative to Congress. A year later, he was chosen to be United States Senator, but he resigned in April, 1798. From 1798 until 1804, he was a judge of the Supreme Court of Tennessee and was also Major-General of the Tennessee militia. These were all high honors for so young a man. But while he was in the Senate, the leaders in the government were shocked by him. They thought his manners were those of a backwoodsman. Even the President of the Senate, Thomas Jefferson, complained about his quarrelsome nature and said, "His passions are terrible." However, one thing was clear to everyone: Andrew Jackson was a spokesman for the common people—the backbone of the new nation. And the people admired and respected him.

19

In 1804 Judge Jackson resigned because he had many heavy debts. Remembering his vow from years before, he was determined to pay them off. So he sold his plantation, Hunter's Hill, and moved with Rachel to a new estate called the Hermitage. There he built a log house of three rooms. With no children of their own, the Jacksons adopted three boys from Rachel's family and named them Jack, Alfred, and Andrew Jackson, Jr. Jackson worked hard at farming and business. In a few years his debts were paid and he had settled down to a quiet life. Not for long, though. The War of 1812 began, and Jackson and his militia were called to action. But after waiting outside Natchez for four weeks, starving and frozen, they were sent home again. Jackson was furious. Using his own money to hire wagons for those too weak to walk, he marched with his troops back to Nashville. "Look at him," said one of his soldiers. "He's as tough as a hickory branch." And from then on Jackson was known as "Old Hickory."

That was not the end of Jackson's military career. It had just gotten started. Soon he led his men into battle against the Creeks, a tribe of Indians who were on the side of the British in the War of 1812. The Creeks had killed many white settlers in the territory just south of Tennessee. Among Jackson's troops were men like Sam Houston and Davy Crockett, who were to become legends in their own right. The final battle ended one day in March, 1814, when the leader of the Creeks walked calmly into Jackson's camp to give himself up. He was Bill Weatherford and he was part English—his Indian name was Red Eagle. He said, "Kill me, if you will." General Jackson offered his hand instead, and upon their handshake the war with the Creeks was won. Word spread in newspapers all over the country. Andrew Jackson was a hero. On his triumphant journey home he carried on his saddle an orphaned Indian boy. He was named Lincoya and was raised with Jackson's other boys.

Not long after Jackson got home, word came that he had been made Major-General of the Regular Army of the United States. The war was still going on and he was needed to protect New Orleans and to keep the British from invading. Already the city of Washington had been captured and the Capitol and the White House burned. At once Jackson led a strange collection of soldiers into New Orleans. There were backwoodsmen, clerks, shopkeepers, Indians, and freed slaves, mixed with French soldiers who had fought the British in Europe. Under Jackson's leadership they fought valiantly and only seven of them died in the decisive battle on January 8, 1815. But the British lost hundreds of men and ten days later they slipped quietly away during the night. Even so, it was a bitter victory. The war had been ended with a peace treaty signed on December 24, 1814, but this news took two and a half months to reach New Orleans. However, though the Battle of New Orleans had not influenced the war's outcome, "Old Hickory" was more of a hero than ever.

Jackson was so popular that he was nominated for President in 1824. He ran against John Quincy Adams, Henry Clay, and William Crawford. Jackson got the most votes, but he did not have a large enough majority of the electoral votes to win. So the House of Representatives had to vote to choose a President. At the last minute Clay withdrew so Adams would get his votes. In exchange, Clay would be appointed Secretary of State by Adams. When Adams won, Jackson felt he had been cheated out of the Presidency. He was fighting mad. Four years later, in 1828, he ran against Adams again. This time it was a vicious smear campaign. Jackson's private life was attacked and the scandal of his marriage was revived in newspapers and pamphlets. Even so, Jackson won the election. But Rachel, who had heart trouble, had died before the election was over. So, bowed with sorrow, "Old Hickory" went alone to Washington to take the oath of office as President.

26

All the Presidents before Jackson had been men of refinement and culture. Now a man with no education—just a rough, common soldier—was the seventh President. But people loved him! On his inauguration day, Washington was full of pioneers, backwoodsmen, old soldiers, and immigrants. They trampled the lawn of the Capitol trying to see him take his oath. Then they swarmed after him as he rode on horseback to the White House. They pushed through the doors and trampled on the carpets in muddy boots. Chairs and settees were broken as men climbed up to get a glimpse of their hero. China and glass were smashed in the East Room as people grabbed the cakes, ice cream, and punch from the long, beautifully arranged tables. Finally Jackson got away from the wild crowd and escaped through a window. He spent the first night of his Presidency in a hotel. There has never been such a ruckus at the White House since that day!

29

During his first term of office, Jackson faced one of the most important questions of his time—could a state refuse to enforce a Federal law? South Carolina had said it would not obey a certain law that Congress had passed. Many people believed that a state had the right to "nullify" a law it didn't like, but Jackson did not agree. He said, "Our Federal Union. It must be preserved." Now people knew that he stood for the whole country, united as one nation. And when South Carolina threatened to leave the Union, or secede, over this problem, Jackson sent warships to Charleston harbor. Then, in a Proclamation, he told the people of South Carolina, "Disunion by armed force is treason." Most of the country cheered its agreement and South Carolina backed down. There would be no war, and no secession. The Union was preserved. Thirty years later, Abraham Lincoln would face this same question and the full price in blood would be paid before it was settled.

Another problem Jackson confronted as President was a many-headed monster called the Second Bank of the United States. This bank was owned by a few wealthy men. The government's money was held in it. This meant that a small number of rich men could control the country's money. The people themselves and their representatives in Congress had no say in how the money should be used. Jackson thought this was wrong. He believed that these few men and their bank with its many branches should not make decisions about the government's money all by themselves. Other people disagreed, especially those who were friends of the Bank's owners and who could borrow money from it whenever they wanted. Many Congressmen also liked the Bank. So they passed a law that said the Bank could continue. But Jackson vetoed—or refused to sign—this law. Then he took the government's money out of the Bank and put it into many smaller banks, where it could be used by more people. After that, the many-headed monster—the Second Bank of the United States—collapsed and died.

33

Just before his second term of office ended, Jackson at age 68 made a tour of the northeast United States. Wherever he went, he was honored as a national hero. When he returned to Washington, he stayed to attend the inauguration in 1837 of the next President, Martin Van Buren. Then Jackson went home to the mansion he had built in 1819 at the Hermitage. In his last years there he kept busy paying his son Andrew, Jr.'s debts. But he also kept his hand in government. For example, he convinced his friend Sam Houston, President of the Republic of Texas, to ask Congress to admit Texas to the Union. But when Congress finally agreed, Sam Houston changed his mind. Jackson sent his son Jack to Texas to urge Houston to reconsider, and Texas joined the United States in March, 1845, just three months before Jackson's death. So, to the end of his long life, Andrew Jackson never stopped looking for ways to serve his country.

❧ Epilogue ❧

Andrew Jackson, who died on June 8, 1845, in his 79th year, was the seventh President of the United States. He was the first President to be born in a log cabin. He literally fought his way to the White House and plunged into the Presidency with both fists swinging. He represented the pioneers in the rough new settlements west of the Appalachians and the working people in the raw and growing cities of the East; there were enough of them to elect him President twice. Jackson's was the era when political cartoons came of age. Maybe it was because his tall, skinny frame, his mop of tangled hair, and his backwoods manners were easy to make fun of. Although some people thought he was crude in many ways, he is now considered one of our greatest Presidents. His faults were many, but he loved his country simply and with all his heart.

36